The author was born in the city of Bristol and has lived there for most of his life. He studied at the City of Bristol College before crossing the Severn Bridge to complete his studies and research at the University of Wales. He is a member of British Association for Counselling and Psychotherapy (BACP).

As a qualified counsellor Andy works with clients with a wide range of problems including addictions, OCD and PTSD using a relational integrative model which supports Cognitive Behavioural, Humanistic and Psychodynamic therapies.

Andy presented the research for this book at the BACP Annual National conference in Liverpool in May 2011.

This book is dedicated with love to Edna and Fred Lansdown

Andrew J Lansdown

THE HUMOUR TRIANGLE

Copyright © Andrew J Lansdown (2014)

The right of Andrew J Lansdown to be identified as author of this work has been asserted by him in accordance with section 77 and 78 of the Copyright, Designs and Patents Act 1988.

All rights reserved. No part of this publication may be reproduced, stored in a retrieval system, or transmitted in any form or by any means, electronic, mechanical, photocopying, recording, or otherwise, without the prior permission of the publishers.

Any person who commits any unauthorized act in relation to this publication may be liable to criminal prosecution and civil claims for damages.

A CIP catalogue record for this title is available from the British Library.

ISBN 978 1 78455 156 8

www.austinmacauley.com

First Published (2014)
Austin Macauley Publishers Ltd.
25 Canada Square
Canary Wharf
London
E14 5LB

Printed and bound in Great Britain

Acknowledgments

With thanks and deep gratitude to Jenny and Becky for their unwavering support and belief.

Thanks to Martin Williamson for his wonderful artwork and for bringing Berkeley and The Prof to life.

'*The Humour Triangle*' is a work of fiction, any resemblance between the characters herein and real persons living or dead is purely coincidental.

Part One

Among the coffee shop, customers occupying the tables fringing the platform, just one wasn't either engrossed with a mobile device or talking to fellow travellers. A middle-aged man was sitting perfectly still and smiling inanely, as if he were watching a private invisible floor show. His obvious enjoyment of an empty spot on the platform deterred other coffee shops clients from invading his personal space or sitting in the vacant seat at his table. Blissfully unaware of the message he was emanating the lone man mentally re-running the previous day's presentation he'd attended at a conference in psychotherapy.

As with all conferences, there was a fringe element, and this one had been no different. At each conference he allowed himself the indulgence of attending just one of the 'off the wall' presentations, for light relief rather than to learn something new. This year he'd chosen one entitled 'Humorous Things Happen in Therapy' half expecting a skit from a colleague with delusions of abandoning his current profession to join the stand-up circuit. Expecting little of entertainment value and certainly no academic worth, the time could be spent answering e-mails, so it was with zero expectations that the Professor of Psychotherapy from a mediocre South Western university, selected a seat near the back of the auditorium and opened up his, now ageing, laptop.

The presenter had opened with a description of the research he'd undertaken, all pretty standard stuff, but no laughs so far. This was not a jester's testing ground, but an attempt at a serious piece of academic work. Nothing in the introduction warranted an upward glance away from the overflowing inbox. But when the newly qualified counsellor boldly claimed that humour could be used in therapy the Professor's attention was drawn to the podium.

Throughout Prof Hawthorn's career there was an unwritten assumption that the use of humour in therapy sessions is strictly taboo. During his teaching career he'd taken pride in being able to spot the students who were able to suppress their humour and therefore better able to become the 'dead pan' reflective personalities ideally suited to the profession. He'd often had to mark down students who had tried to interject humour into their work and sessions, as the use of humour in any form in therapy sessions was considered not only to be bad taste but potentially dangerous to the client/therapist relationship.

But here was a guy, not a youngster by any stretch of the imagination, advocating the adoption of a 'method' by which humour could be safely used in the consulting room. He spoke of a 'Humour Triangle' as a tool by which humour could be used to lighten the mood and relax communication during sensitive therapy sessions.

The presenter, a guy called Lansdown, was telling the audience that the purpose of his research was to establish if the use of humour, by the therapist, would enhance or inhibit the therapeutic relationship. He'd conducted a small scale research project consisting of five interviews with established therapists and a questionnaire completed by twenty-five final year student therapists.

The feedback he'd received prompted a unique leap in thought and it became obvious that before humour could be used in therapy, there were three distinct obstacles that had to be overcome to guarantee success. The first of these was the use of an appropriate (or inappropriate) type of humour... sarcasm, irony, puns, stories; for example a client whose first language is not English may not have the linguistic skills to appreciate ironic jokes, or humorous metaphors. He identified this as *Clarification: an understanding of the type of humour an individual client would appreciate.* The second obvious potential stumbling block was the ability of the therapist to interject appropriate concepts in the humour; an extreme example being the use of death as a subject matter to a grieving spouse. *The ability to find the right springboard he described as Identification.* The third and final obstacle the research identified, was the ability of the therapists to time their humorous interjections to ensure that a beneficial reaction is experienced by both participants, such as relieving the pressure at a difficult point in the session, thereby contributing to the positive building of the client therapist relationship. Not surprisingly, Lansdown labelled this element of his trifecta as *Timing: which every comedian will openly admit is the golden key to good comedy.*

Lansdown worked these three elements into 'The Humour Triangle': Clarification; Identification and Timing. He boldly postulated that providing all three were present in the right form or quantity, then humour could be considered as a useful intervention tool in the therapeutic process, which would allow the relationship to mature.

Lansdown stated very clearly from the outset that 'The Humour Triangle' was not a formula for telling jokes and quite rightly pointed out that joke telling in the therapy session would have a high probability of ending in disaster for the therapist.

Over the years Professor Hawthorn had attended many seminars, but this presentation was different and he began to wonder whether it could be that this guy, Lansdown, had come up with an acceptable formula that therapists could actually use. The title of Lansdown's presentation suggested that humorous things *do happen* in therapy and he could confirm this from personal experiences, however, not many therapists mention in conversation "Oh by the way, a funny thing happened in therapy today" – after all the Professor had assumed that it was taboo for therapists to use humour in therapy sessions. Lansdown had grabbed his attention and the model of the humour triangle stayed with him long after the conference ended.

As a supervisor to other established therapists, Professor Hawthorn could not recount even one of them mentioning the use of humour as an intervention with a client. However, Lansdown's presentation had left a mark on his thoughts and he was left wanting more information. His eyes were drawn to the image of a Triangle on the handout that had been distributed at the beginning of the presentation. It looked so simple, but could it really be as effective as Lansdown claimed? Not solely convinced humour was a good approach to use in therapy, Professor Hawthorn thought about how he might put The Humour Triangle to the test and decided to share it with his long-time friend, Berkeley Squire, a successful stand-up comedian with a demanding after dinner speaking schedule and a full diary of bookings for cruise liners, who relished the interaction with live audiences.

His thoughts were broken by the announcement of his trains' departure and he quickly bundled up his belongings and just made it to the compartment on time. Once settled in his seat the Professor sent a text to Berkeley and explained that he would like his friend to take a look at Lansdown's presentation and it was sent through the ether before he settled down to grade e-papers during the rest of his journey home.

The following Sunday the Professor and Berkeley met up for their regular lunchtime pint to discuss Lansdown's hypothesis. Over the years the two friends had taken an interest in each other's professions, sharing literature and biographies of the heroes' of their own fields.

"This 'Humour Triangle' is interesting, but not much more than any good comic will tell you Prof. I'm in no doubt that if all the principles of it are present then, in my oh so humble opinion, I would be confident that even in your staid hands, humour could work, but, I'm a comedian and that's my job; you're a therapist so I'm not sure how well therapists and humour complement each other."

"I see what you are saying Berkeley, but if you remember Lemma [1] said that, a stand-up comedian who fails to be funny and 'dies a death' is very like a therapist who uses an inappropriate humorous intervention which could potentially damage the therapeutic relationship."

"Yeah, that guy hit the nail on the head, it is an awful experience to die the death on stage and he was also aware, as is every stand-up I know, it's virtually impossible to win a whole audience over once you have upset some of them."

"So how do you prevent this from happening?"

Berkeley almost snorted beer out of his nose as his friends' seemingly simple question. Once he'd regained his composure and his friend had stopped laughing at his schoolboy-like actions he said, "If I knew the answer to this, I would have the answer to the meaning of life!"

The quizzical look on the Professor's face made it clear that he wanted him to expand on this sweeping statement "Humour comes in many different shapes and forms and can be interpreted many different ways, so there is no one simple answer, but what I would say is that each audience is different and we have to be careful to find out what kind of audience they are likely to be and then prepare acts to suit. We comics make it look easy but I can tell you there is much more to our job than meets the eye. We spend hours, writing, adjusting and trying out material and even then it won't suit all audiences which means that, at times we have to change things 'on the fly' if we are beginning to bomb."

Still frowning the Professor said, "So identifying your audience is critical."

"Absolutely," replied Berkeley, "no way would I be telling anti-royalist jokes in front of the Queen."

The Professor nodded and thought of the reference Clarkson [2] had written:

'Humour obviously needs to be used with care and only where the relationship is already established and the psychotherapist has some evidence of the patient's ability to tolerate humour'

The Professor went on, "OK, going back to 'The Humour Triangle' model in relation to comedy, having established 'Identification' is critical, how do you establish the relationship with an audience?"

"Like I said, I have to be very careful and this is where the second principle comes into play as a comedian. I must 'Clarify' that the audience will understand what type of humour I intend to use – let me give you an example: I've identified you're a therapist and also a professor, so already I have clarified that you would understand and respond to humour surrounding your profession. Here's the example:

The aspiring therapists were attending their first class on emotional extremes. "Just to establish some parameters," said the professor to the student from Arkansas, "What is the opposite of joy?"

"Sadness," said the student.

And the opposite of depression?" he asked of the young lady from Oklahoma.

"Elation," said she.

"And you sir," he said to the young man from Texas, "how about the opposite of woe?"

The Texan replied, "Sir, I believe that would be giddy-up."

"Very funny," said the Prof laughing out loud, "but how did you know I would be amused by this? I might be very serious and not like the idea of this student making me look silly in front of the rest of the class."

Berkeley agreed that this could have been the case but he had already weighed up their long-standing relationship and there was a 2 to 1 chance that Prof would find this funny, and as the joke was about American students, no offence could be taken by a British Professor.

"Only 2 to 1, I don't like those chances," exclaimed the Professor, "how can I get better odds?"

Berkley pointed to the humour triangle: "Look here Prof; Lansdown has got it right; Identification and Clarification alone will not guarantee that humour will be successful. If the 'Timing' is right, then you have every chance that it will work. So in this instance, 'The Humour Triangle' does hold credence as all three elements were present. You were ready for a joke to lighten the mood. And don't forget, you know I'm a comedian, so like my audiences you are always expecting a few throw away lines from me to pepper our conversations, and when I perform on stage my audience know that I'm going to try to make them laugh, that's what they have paid for and why after dinner, speaking is so much fun. I'm playing to a roomful of people who are gathered together because of a single interest. They are a gift."

The Professor thought about this for a while, Berkeley was right, knowing that he is a comedian sets the expectation levels of anyone he is with...

they expect him to make them laugh, but as therapists we won't have that expectation so a joke coming 'out of the blue' has to be even better prepared than Berkeley's stand-up routine.

As though he was reading the Professors thoughts Berkeley continued, "But for you 'timing' is even more critical as your 'audience' is not expecting to walk out of a session with you crying tears of laughter."

They wrestled with the issue of managing clients' expectations for a while, then Berkeley expanded on the fact that humour can be interpreted in many different ways and can cause harm as well as lightening the mood. "You know Prof, I've had people write to me, and tell me in person, that my show has brought them out of depression or given them a different view on life. When I ask them to pinpoint what helped them the most, they almost always pick a joke or story I've told that gave them a different life view of a problem they'd been dogged by." After a few seconds of silence between them Berkeley continued.

"You see, I do listen to you and often think of those old Greek guys you admire so much who spouted that good humour is an essential part of good health and well being, especially when I get that kind of feedback. But, I bet they didn't quite understand how powerful the surprise of a well thought out and timed punch line can really be."

The Prof snapped out of his thoughts and added, "Ah, perhaps the Greeks hadn't quite caught on to the idea of how effective a well thought out twist in the tale of a joke can be, but, do you remember me mentioning a therapist called Suls [3] who came up with a theory which he called the 'Incongruity Resolution Model'?"

"Yeah, I read that and thought that all he'd done was given a good punch line a fancy name!"

"In a way you're right; his observation was quite simple and elegant, as all the best ideas are. If an audience are able to predict the end of a joke, then the chances are the humour may not work as well as the presenter would like, in fact as Lemma suggested, he could metaphorically die on stage. However, what Sul's suggested, was that if the audience is surprised with a punch line they're not expecting, then the humour used will in his words 'cause laughter'. Let me give you an example:

A Therapist got home from work and his wife said - 'I'm very sorry dear, but the cat's eaten your dinner'.

The expected ending would be 'never mind I'll have something else to eat', which is no surprise. However the punch line is:

'Don't worry - I'll get you a new cat'

Berkeley let out a roaring laugh much to the Professor's surprise adding, "I'm going to steal that joke if, that's OK with you Prof."

"Of course, if you like it that much."

See how using Sul's Incongruity Resolution Model, you the receiver of humour, will see something in a new light? Thinking about it, this is because the humour gives another insight or interpretation to the situation, exactly what we as therapists are trying to get many of our clients to do as part of the healing process."

Berkeley thought about this and realised that this was true of the audience members he'd met who had thanked him for helping them. They'd been stuck in a groove and his humour helped them 'break out' of a particular way a thinking, which was what took most people into therapy in the first place.

The Professor quoted another therapist, Martin [4], who was also was a supporter of Sul's, and was very fond of one of his sayings which to him epitomised humour:

'That the aspects of jokes that are usually thought to be aggressive and disparaging are not really aggressive, but instead are a way of providing the information needed for the incongruity to be resolved.'

Berkeley concluded, "So the best punch-line is one that quickly and clearly paints an unexpected picture in the mind's eye of the listener.

As a comedian I sometimes have to exaggerate humour, like a cartoonist who exaggerates his characters. That allows the reader to see a clearer picture of what the cartoonist is trying to express. So I can see how Lansdown's 'Humour Triangle' would indeed be a good learning catalyst for anyone, let alone a therapist, to work with humour.

In fact any budding comedian should be aware of the three principles of 'The Humour Triangle' because if it is used correctly, it will allow humour to be used in the way intended and let's face it, when we think of humour it is not just about telling jokes as humour comes in many different guises.

As Lansdown suggested, humorous things DO happen in therapy. I would think the bigger question would be: 'can humour improve or inhibit the therapeutic process?'

"That's the big question my friend. Let's see if a little more liquid inspiration can help us unravel this mystery, shall we?" said The Professor as he picked up the empty glasses and moved towards the bar.

When their third pint glasses were empty the men went their separate ways. Hawthorn was deep in thought as he walked home. Lansdown had reminded him of the Winston Churchill quote 'A joke is a serious thing' and in many ways this statement encapsulates the use of humour in counselling therapy, where it can be beneficial in terms of relationship building, but also potentially detrimental if the humour is misunderstood.

But surely Lansdown had a valid point – humorous things *do happen* in therapy. So how, as therapists, do we react when this happens? What protection do we have if humour backfires? Unlike Berkeley, who could get another gig, a therapist runs the risk of being hauled in front of the British Association of Counselling & Psychotherapists

(BACP) for not upholding the ethical framework which all member therapists must strive to work within.

Prof recalled the opening of Lansdown's presentation – he challenged his audience, right at the beginning by saying, 'Anyone who says humorous thing do not happen in the therapy room is being economical with the truth.' Everyone present was aware of what he was suggesting – there is an elephant in the room but no one wants to mention it. This statement seemed to resonate with everyone in the room as it fell eerily silent.

As therapists, once we acknowledge the elephant's existence then we can begin to work with it, metaphorically speaking, but as an experienced therapist the reality is once clients recognise the existence of their problem then it becomes possible that both therapist and client can work together and resolve it. Berkeley was right; humour is a good way of drawing out an issue and discovering the reality of it. Humour can also help to see a problem from a different perspective. But, could Lansdown's 'Humour Triangle' really give therapists' the confidence to work with humour when the right opportunity arises? For this to happen successfully it would be necessary to have some safe and practical guidelines, so, perhaps 'The Humour Triangle' is the tool needed to do this. After all, triangles are known to be very stable, but had this guy really hit upon a new therapy tool?

In order to test this new thought the Prof decided to look into the practicality of using 'The Humour Triangle' as a Module in Therapy Training to help therapists work with clients when humorous things happen, after all a therapist should not shy away from what is a natural form of communication for most of us and humour has been central to human communication, so there should be a way to integrate it to therapy sessions. This thought brought the Professor back to 'those Greek guys', as Berkeley referred to them, and the writings of Woolfe [5] who said humour can be traced back to the ancient Greek society where good health depended on the balance of the 'humours', literally meaning a 'balance of health.' Prof chuckled, if it was good enough for the Greeks, then it should be good enough for a modern day therapist to use.

Over the coming days Professor Hawthorn was being drawn to Lansdown's idea, but humour hadn't been taught as a therapeutic intervention. How on earth would one write a lesson plan for teaching the use of humour? He decided to do a little more research about the reported effects humour can have in the consulting room. There were ample arguments for both its use and avoidance. However, using the three principles of 'The Humour Triangle,' to make sure that humour is only used when all three are in balance, it was possible to see that there is a solid middle ground that could produce a precedence allowing the use of humour in sessions where it would have a good chance to add value.

During the Q&A portion of his presentation Lansdown was asked if he thought that therapists could be struck off for using humour as a therapeutic tool. "Yes, however we are not talking about telling jokes, we are talking about responding to humorous things that the client bring to the session." His response at the time did not quite ring true, but now he'd had time to absorb more information and opinions on the subject, the response Lansdown gave made more sense. "Clarification, Identification and Timing; when these are recognised by the therapist, and used as a therapeutic model they will give a significant indication as to whether humour will be beneficial."

Lansdown qualified this by adding, "I strongly suggest that if one of the three principles is missing, then humour will not be useful and could potentially, damage the relationship between therapist and client. My premise is based upon the fact that humour can be useful but we must be very aware that it could be inappropriate.

If you are making particular reference to the principles of beneficence and non-malfeasance; the guidelines state very clearly that the therapist's role is to promote the client's well-being and to avoid harm to the client. Applying the three principles of 'The Humour Triangle' will not violate these guidelines, in fact it should make it easier and safer to introduce humour as an intervention tool, and still adhere to the BACP ethical framework."

With this in mind, Professor Hawthorn was convinced that the principles of 'The Humour Triangle' could allow a therapist to enter in to well modulated, humorous dialogue with a client. These fundamental principles should be considered in all interventions, in fact Lansdown's Humour Triangle was not only simple to understand, but he had actually given a concrete platform for all therapists to work from.

Professor Hawthorn had witness many trainee therapists' struggle with interventions, but now, if they could utilize a quick check list, using 'The Humour Triangle', it might help them resolve their issues. He had always stressed to his students that therapy is primarily about the client and as therapists they should always beware of this during therapy sessions; that at all times they should maintain their focus on their clients' needs and maintain a strong awareness of how their own beliefs can detract from this focus.

What Lansdown had demonstrated was that the Triangle could be applied to a very wide range of communication tools; it was just that Lansdown had hit upon 'The Humour Triangle' when assessing the use of humour.

Everyone admits to having a sense of humour, but we all also have a complex web of beliefs and perspectives and it is the job of the therapist to give their clients the emotional space they need to explore their problems using a dizzying array of communication formats, but until now there hadn't been a single model that gave the therapists a quick check to make sure they are right in their assumptions to use a specific mode of communication.

After more Sunday sessions with Berkeley, Professor Hawthorn concluded that their professions of therapist and comedian are not as diverse as they had initially assumed. Their own friendship had grown out of a shared interest in human communication and as long as therapists were aware of their own sense of humour, as Berkley indicated, reiterating the fact that something funny to one person may not be funny to his audience/client and handled incorrectly, the effects can be disastrous.

The more they tested 'The Humour Triangle' the more they became convinced that it was valid – for any form of communication.

Part Two

Despite his best efforts, the Professor was still struggling to construct a lesson plan on how to teach the use of humour and decided to go to the source and invited Lansdown to give his presentation at his university.

On the appointed day the auditorium was full to capacity and some latecomers were surprised to find that they had to stand or sit on the steps that ran down each side of the room. The Professor was watching with interest as the students and some of his colleagues entered. It was obvious from their reaction that his regular students were as surprised as he was at the number of people attending this one-off presentation for a visiting lecturer. As the time approached to start the Professor stepped up to the lectern and called for the attention of the assembled academics.

"Thank you all for coming here today to hear what should be a very interesting and thought provoking presentation." Scanning the room he let his gaze fall on the core of students sitting towards the front of the audience and addressed them.

"As students of our subject you are sometimes daunted by the complexity of our chosen field of study, psychotherapy. You will be expected to study and recount the work of many prominent therapists whose methodologies you will hopefully use during your future careers. And while you will be tested on tried and trusted ways to assist your clients, you may feel that there is no more room for new ideas or tools within our profession. Today you will see that this is not necessarily so. There may be 'nothing new on heaven or earth', but today you will see that there are new ways to view the world in which we and our clients live and function. Our presenter today is Mr. Andy Lansdown, who has recently qualified as a Therapist and who for part of his training undertook the study of a facet of our work that is considered to be taboo, that is the use of Humour in Therapy sessions.

I suspect that, as I did when I first encountered the title of this presentation, that Andy might be offering us amusing anecdotes about things that happen in therapy sessions, but you will see that he has undertaken a serious study of this subject and as he puts it, has been brave enough to acknowledge the 'elephant in the room'. I hope you will find this as thought provoking as I did and that you will recognize that there is always room for new ideas in our profession and that you as future therapists can make a contribution to our field."

Lansdown approached the lectern and thanked the Professor for the opportunity to share his findings with his students.

"Does anyone here know any good jokes?"

The underlying hubbub of whispered conversations ceased, leaving complete silence. No one wanted their talking to be mistaken for an offer to tell a joke in front of such a large audience.

"You have given me the perfect response. Let me ask you, why are none of you prepared to stand up and tell us all a joke?"

One student raised her hand slowly. Lansdown nodded at her, "Because people might not laugh."

"Exactly! Thank you. Whether we are conducting a therapy session or in the pub with our friends, we have an inbuilt instinct that tells us if it is the right time or appropriate to tell a joke, admittedly if alcohol is involved we may be less inhibited, but all the same we have to gauge if the joke we are about to tell will backfire and make us look foolish. We instinctively assess if our seemingly funny contribution to the conversation will result in the response we are seeking, laughter.

As we know humour is a two sided event so when humorous things happen in a therapy session, how are we expected to react? If the client is the instigator of the 'joke', how should we react, especially if the client is attempting to use humour to depreciate his or her self? As therapists, should we laugh at a witty self put-down if our client is suffering from low self-esteem? Probably not advisable, would you agree? Moreover, can we use humour to help our clients gain a better understanding or viewpoint of their situation?

Remembering what Winston Churchill said, 'A joke is serious thing' and it is from this viewpoint, that I want to introduce to you the principles of 'The Humour Triangle', a tool that therapists or indeed anyone can use to engage in humorous exchanges with confidence.

In short, what I want to demonstrate to you today is that humorous exchanges between a client and therapist can enhance the therapeutic relationship and in doing so allow the client to examine an issue from a different viewpoint.

Before I move on to the more practical side of my theory I need to address a very big issue. During my training the premise that a joke is a serious thing was emphasised time and time again and although the British Association of Counselling and Psychotherapists don't exactly state that the use of humour is a no-go area, the distinct impression we, as trainees, get is that the use of humour in therapy is taboo.

The BACP might consider that the use of humour could be perceived, by the client, to be derogatory or a way of poking fun at their predicament, so it is conceivable that used in this way it could be seen as a violation of the ethical principles and at the very least inappropriate and possibly unprofessional.

I agree with this premise and would not endorse the use of humour IF the client might consider it to be inappropriate. But, how can we as therapists know if our clients will take offence at our attempts to introduce humour? This may seem like an unanswerable question and one that prompted the basis of my research to find out if humour can be used a positive therapeutic tool; can humour enhance or inhibit the therapeutic relationship?"

At this point Lansdown stopped talking for a few beats, while a low level buzz of conversation engulfed the room. The Professor spied some of his colleagues contributing to the buzz as they turned sideways to pass comments to each other. One thing was obvious; Lansdown had been able to command the attention of the audience, just as he had at the conference. The Professor experienced an unexpected wave of relief as he realised that both his students and colleagues were as interested in what Lansdown had to say, as he had been.

Lansdown cleared his throat to continue and the buzz subsided.

"When I submitted this subject title for consideration for my dissertation, it was met with some puzzlement, prompting comments along the lines of 'this is perhaps too creative and unusual a subject for you to undertake'.

After revising and submitting my proposal a couple of times I was finally given the go ahead. Not long after I received this news I bumped into one of the lecturers from my undergraduate days who asked how I was doing. I briefly explained that my proposal had just been accepted and her immediate response was 'You're having a laugh, aren't you?' She obviously thought I was joking but when I said, 'No', she looked bewildered and said, 'Lansdown, you are totally dyslexic, colour blind and just for good measure short sighted', all of which are true, and continued, "good luck, if anyone can pull this off you can. I've always admired your creativity, even if it has been a little close to the mark at times, which I suspect your peers in your Personal Development Group, will attest'. We both laughed and as she began to walk away she turned and said, 'On a final note I will warn you that you will meet with some heavy criticism on this research journey, but I'd urge you not to give up and I, for one, will be looking forward to reading your findings'.

With this mixed endorsement ringing in my ears I set up interviews with various therapists to discuss the question 'Have you ever considered using humour as an intervention tool with a client?'

Of course I need to protect the anonymity of the therapists I interviewed, but I can assure you that the responses I got were as mixed as the reaction of my undergraduate lecturer. I got both affirmative and negative responses and one therapist I interviewed, that I travelled for four hours to meet up with, was scathing to the point of anger despite the fact that she had been very keen to participate in my research. She obviously thought that I needed to be taught a lesson as she berated me for even thinking that humour could be used in therapy sessions. During our meeting her dog was sat at her side and contributed to my tongue lashing by interjecting snarls when his mistress's voice hit a certain pitch and volume. I must say that the combined effect was disconcerting, and even more so when the dog bared its teeth and appeared to be sniggering at my questions until it began to emit a low pitched growl, a trick that I am sure the therapists would have performed herself, if she could have.

Having escaped with my physical being in one piece I was able to put a very firm tick in the No column of my research.

There were other interviews that balanced this view with as much 'enthusiasm' as the dog lady, and on the whole I ended up with a fairly even split of 'For' and 'Against' votes for the use of therapy as an intervention tool.

Of course there was much more to my findings than an fairly even split, and to demonstrate to you the complexities behind the polar arguments I would like you to participate in a mock trial, where I will, unconventionally, present evidence for both sides of the argument and let you decide if humour should or should not be used in therapy."

Lansdown's last statement seemed to stimulate the students interest as they all scrabbled about to find note paper and pens, some even closing their laptops to give what would follow their full attention.

As the Professor scanned the assembled group he noticed a newcomer at the back, it was Berkeley, his friend. He'd forgotten he'd invited Berkeley to the session, as the invitation was made quite flippantly and without any expectation that it would be taken up.

Over the next thirty minutes Lansdown presented a very cogent, well researched and interesting array of 'evidence' from luminaries in the field of psychotherapy and their views on the use of humour.

What Might happen if Humour is accepted as a Therapeutic Tool?	
The use of Humour can Enhance the Client/Therapist relationship if:	**The use of Humour can Inhibit the Client/Therapist relationship if:**
<ul><li>The therapist senses that it will be useful to use humour.</li><li>A shared appreciated humour can enhance the counselling relationship.</li><li>It allows client to see that the therapist has a sense of humour.</li><li>It can show that the therapist as a real person and not an aloof counsellor.</li><li>It can help the client become more aware of, or rediscover, their own sense of humour.</li></ul>	<ul><li>The therapist loses confidence when a humorous intervention backfires.</li><li>The humour is misinterpreted as flirting with a client.</li><li>The client thinks the therapist is not taking the therapeutic process seriously.</li><li>The client may think the therapist is laughing at them.</li><li>The therapist comes across as unprofessional.</li><li>The therapist is using humour to enhance their own position.</li><li>Therapeutic work degenerates into a light hearted banter and loses focus on the session.</li><li>The use of humour results in self-disclosure from therapist.</li><li>The client thinks they are not being taken seriously.</li><li>The therapist comes across as a clown or comedian.</li></ul>
The use of Humour can provide Opportunities within the Client/Therapist relationship if:	**The use of Humour can be a Threat to the Client/Therapist relationship if:**
<ul><li>The humour can act as an 'ice breaker'.</li><li>The therapists can be trained on how to deliver humorous interventions.</li><li>It can reflect a depth of understanding of the client by the therapist, enhancing the client/therapist relationship.</li><li>It can help the client to view a problem or situation from another viewpoint.</li></ul>	<ul><li>The therapist is not confident that the use of humour would be beneficial to the client.</li><li>The subject matter of the humour is not appropriate.</li><li>The timing of the humour used is inappropriate.</li></ul>

He was able to draw up this table, loosely based on a SWOT Analysis[1]:

Towards the end of the mock trial Lansdown deviated from the usual summarization for both sides and continued, "I am now going to summarize both sides of this argument with a single summary and one important question."

After a pause to allow the audience to settle down he began his summary "During my research I also asked interviewees the question 'Do you have a sense of humour?' They all said they do. So the question that then begged to be asked was, 'If humour is a natural part of human communication why shouldn't it be used in therapy?' After further discussion the response, almost unanimously, was, 'I've never really thought about it' and 'I don't know how to.' This brings us back to the first question I asked you and the response of the young lady in the front row. If we are uncertain of the outcome we will receive from our clients we will not risk upsetting them? So, the question I'm asking you to vote upon is:

'If there were a way we could safely use humour in therapy sessions could we, or even, should we?'

I'd like to take a vote now and see how we stand on this issue. When you vote, remember that under the BAPC ethical framework we have a duty to commit to promoting our clients well-being and to avoid doing any harm.

---

[1] A quartered framework into which the Strengths, Weaknesses, Opportunities and Threats are listed and compared.

As we are scheduled to take a short break could you write your vote on a slip of paper and drop them in the box just outside the main door and we will reconvene in fifteen minutes. Thank you."

As the buzz of conversation returned to the room, Berkeley and some of the staff made their way to the podium and the Prof met him and left Lansdown to talk to the staff members interested in getting the inside track on the final part of his presentation.

"So, what do you think of it so far?" asked the Prof.

"I had no idea that this was such a contentious issue for you guys. That analysis he put up was really loaded towards the negatives wasn't it? Jokes really are a serious thing for you aren't they?"

"Yes, as teachers we are always trying to make sure we're not letting our students into the profession without realizing what a heavy burden of responsibility they are taking on, and I'm afraid to say it's the jokes and humour that tend to get slapped down the most in training sessions. I guess in a way I'm glad to see that they take it to heart, but in another way I think it's a shame that we can't somehow bring some of the therapeutic values of humour into our work and experience what you do with your breakthroughs. I'm so pleased you are beginning to see how pivotal this issue is in our profession, and perhaps why I sometimes envy your ability to make people laugh, when most of the time I'm working with so much distress and misery."

"Yeah, I guess you can hardly break out into laughter with your clients, even though in some cases laughter might be the best medicine."

"So you really do get it! There are times when I would love to crack a joke with my clients to alleviate the tension or to help them see a situation from another view point. To me that's the potential value of humour in therapy sessions. The punch line of jokes, as you have so often told me, can be a quick way to flip our world view of a subject or situation. A joke can do this in seconds, where I can sometimes invest hours and hours with a client to get the same result!"

"I can see what you are saying now and why this guy's idea has sparked such an interest in you. I missed the first part of his presentation – has he mentioned the triangle yet?"

"Very briefly, not in detail, but I can see where he's going with this. He's hoping that the vote is going to show that if humour can be used safely then it should be an acceptable tool to use. Quite a neat way to present it."

As the audience filed back into the room the votes were collected and counted. The results were handed to Lansdown.

"OK guys, thanks for voting, here are the results," the hall fell silent.

"Over eighty percent of you said it was OK to use humour in therapy.

Twenty percent were not sure …

And not one No voting slip."

Lansdown took a couple of breaths before continuing, perhaps to relish that the outcome of the vote was as he'd expected it to be. He'd got the three elements of the Triangle right!

"I would like to say how I'm amazed that some of you have been able to write short essays on the back of the voting slips, in such a short time, most of which highlight the fact that is not the why or where but the HOW that has you steering clear of introducing humour into your sessions."

The buzz of conversation retuned to room as soon as Lansdown stopped talking. He had to raise his voice to regain their attention.

"So, it would seem that you would be comfortable using humour as an intervention IF YOU KNEW HOW TO DO IT?"

There were nods all around the auditorium. On the screen a large four coloured triangle was projected.

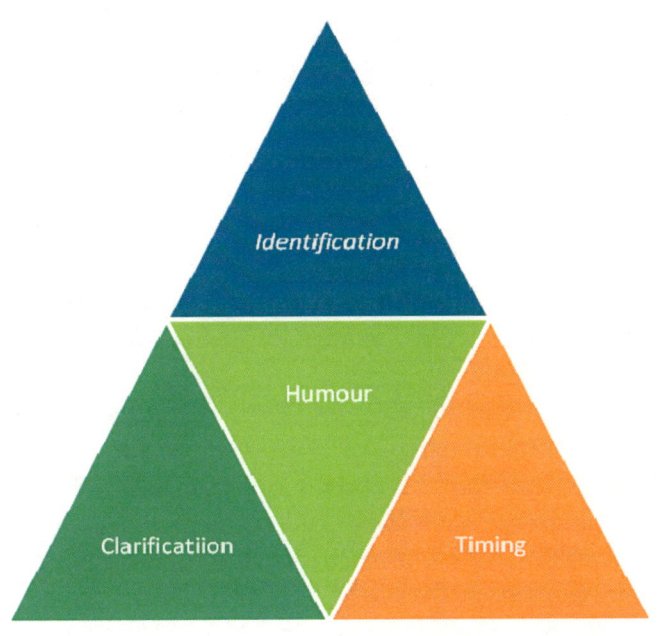

"Funny you should say that… Let me introduce you to 'The Humour Triangle'". Lansdown went on to explain the three principles of **identification** of the subject of humour, **clarification** of the right type of joke and the critical issue of **timing** "And as we work through these three elements try to remember a time when you introduced humour to a conversation and it did not work as you had expected…try to pinpoint which one of the three principles of the Humour Triangle were missing…"

References

[1] LEMMA, A. (2000 p, ix) *Humour on the couch.* Whurr Publishers.

[2] CLARKSON, P. (2003 p 87) *The Therapeutic Relationship* 2nd edn. Whurr Publishers London and Philadelphia

[3] SULS, J. M. (1972) *A two-stage model for the appreciation of jokes and cartoons: An information-processing analysis.* In J. H. Goldstein & P.E. McGee (Eds), *The Psychology of Humour. Theoretical Perspectives and Empirical Issues* (pp81-100) New York: Academic Press. In MARTIN, R. (2007p 65) *The Psychology of Humour an Integrative Approach.* Academic Press Publications.

SULS, J.M. (1977) *Cognitive and disparagement theories of humour: A theoretical and empirical synthesis.* In A. J. Chapman & H.C. Foot (Eds), *It's a funny thing humour* (pp 41-45) Oxford: Pergamon Press. In MARTIN, R. 2007p 66) *The Psychology of Humour an Integrative Approach.* Academic press publications

[4] MARTIN, R.(2007 pp 343,335,337) *The Psychology of Humour an Integrative Approach.* Academic press publications

[5] WOOLFE, R. STRAWBRIDGE, S. DOUGLAS, B. DRYDEN, W. (2010 p37) *Handbook of counselling psychology 3rd edn.* Sage London

Discovering Dyslexia – A Note from the Author

Two dyslexic men walk into a bank shouting...
"Air in the hands mother stickers this is a ***ckup!"

When I was finally tested positive for dyslexia I was told that I was not only totally visually dyslexic but suffer from audio dyslexia as well, which is not at all common. Understandably I was in shock at this news and quietly cried a little as I never knew I was so severely disabled.

I asked my tester what I could do about this and the answer I received back was extremely encouraging and reassuring. These words will stay with me for the rest of my life. "Dyslexia is not a disability, but is an incredible ability to be creative and in your case we can be thankful, as we would never have found this communication tool: The Humour Triangle."